The Lord's Prayer

words taken from Matthew 6:9-13
illustrated by Joan Hutson

© 1983 by Joan Hutson
Published by The STANDARD PUBLISHING Company, Cincinnati, Ohio
Division of STANDEX INTERNATIONAL Corporation. Printed in U.S.A.
The distinctive trade dress of this book is proprietary to Western Publishing Company, Inc., used with permission.

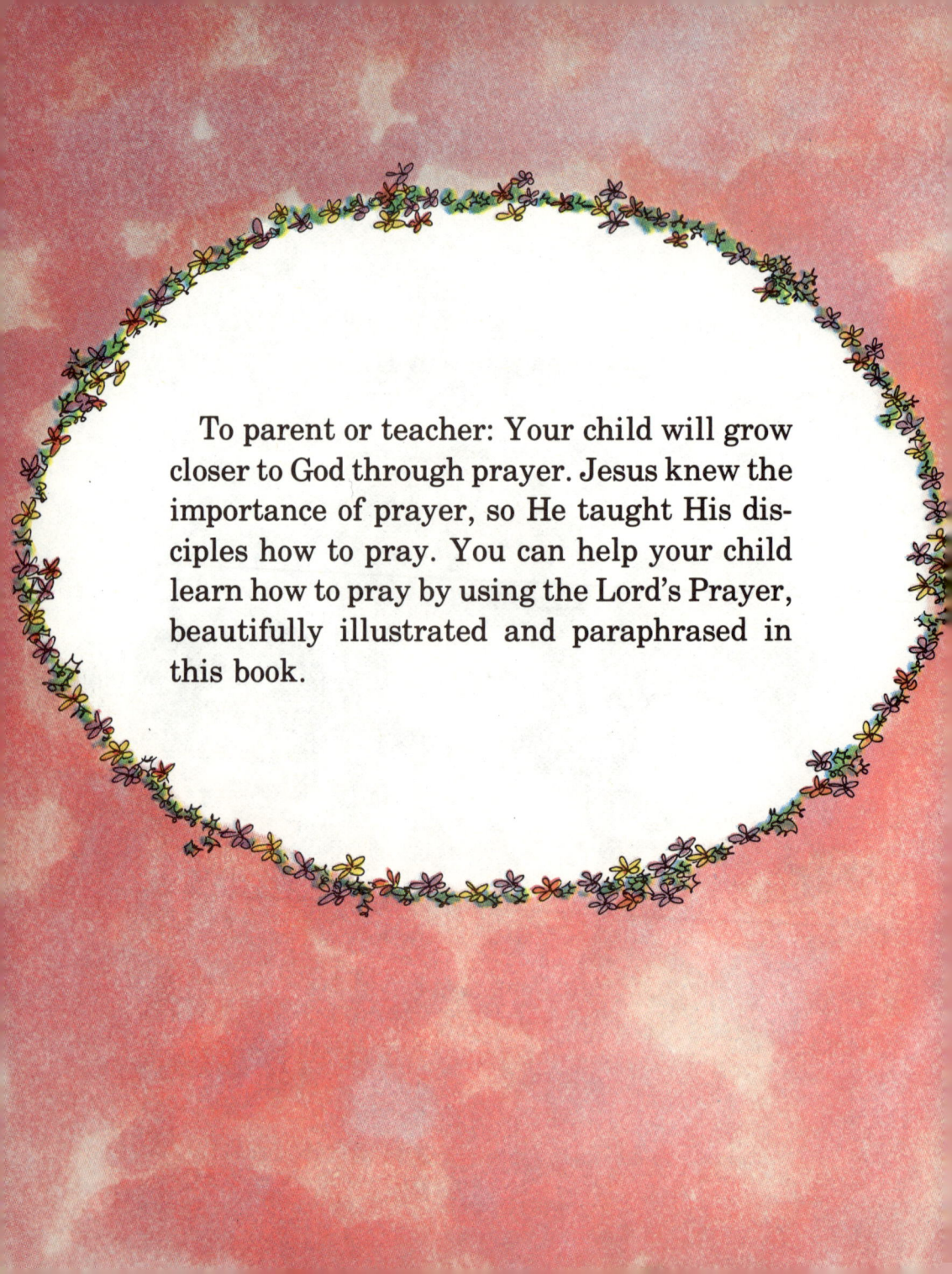

To parent or teacher: Your child will grow closer to God through prayer. Jesus knew the importance of prayer, so He taught His disciples how to pray. You can help your child learn how to pray by using the Lord's Prayer, beautifully illustrated and paraphrased in this book.

Jesus taught His disciples to pray.

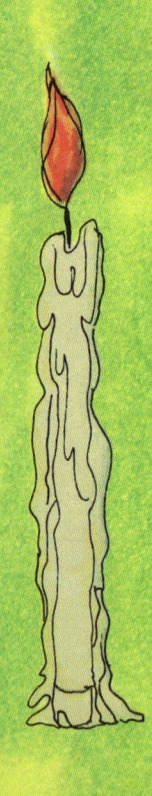

Our Father who art in Heaven,

Jesus said that we should call You our Father.
That means You are mine, and I am yours.

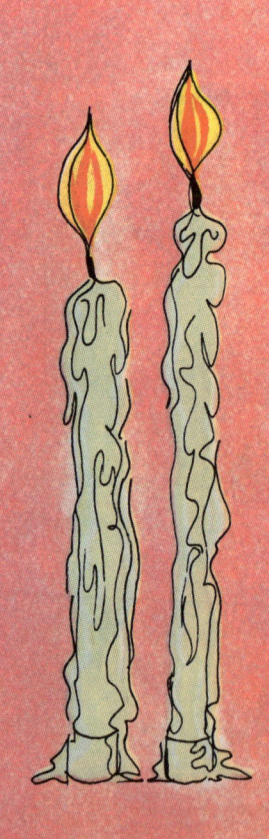

Hallowed be Thy name.

By every voice, from every land, holy, praised, and honored be Your name!

Thy kingdom come.

In all things I must be willing to let You be king of my world as You are king of Heaven.

Thy will be done on earth as it is in Heaven.

In all things, I must be ready to live for You right now.

Give us this day our daily bread.

You give me all I need to love and serve
You faithfully every day of my life.

And forgive us our trespasses,

I know that when I say "Forgive me, Father," You instantly and completely forgive me.

As we forgive those who trespass against us.

I know that when others hurt me, I must instantly and completely forgive them.

And lead us not into temptation, but deliver us from evil:

I know that I must stay away from what can easily lead me into wrong. I know that I must, through prayer, fight against evil.

For thine is the kingdom, and the power, and the glory for ever and ever.

I know that with the saints and angels above, I can join my voice in their chorus of love.

Amen.

The word "amen" means, "Yes, I agree!" When I say it at the end of my prayer, I know I must live the words of my prayer.

THE LORD'S PRAYER

OUR FATHER WHO ART IN HEAVEN
HALLOWED BE THY NAME,
THY KINGDOM COME, THY WILL BE DONE
ON EARTH AS IT IS IN HEAVEN.
GIVE US THIS DAY OUR DAILY BREAD
AND FORGIVE US OUR TRESPASSES
AS WE FORGIVE THOSE WHO TRESPASS AGAINST US
AND LEAD US NOT INTO TEMPTATION
BUT DELIVER US FROM EVIL.
FOR THINE IS THE KINGDOM AND THE POWER
AND THE GLORY FOREVER. AMEN.

MATTHEW 6